dabblelab

PROJECT PASSION

SHARE the Love

Projects You'll Love to Give

by Mari Bolte

CAPSTONE PRESS
a capstone imprint

Dabble Lab is published by Capstone Press,
1710 Roe Crest Drive, North Mankato, Minnesota 56003
www.mycapstone.com

Library of Congress Cataloging-in-Publication Data is available
on the Library of Congress website.

ISBN: 978-1-5157-7374-0 (library hardcover)
ISBN: 978-1-5157-7378-8 (eBook PDF)

Editorial Credits:
Kayla Rossow, designer; Tori Abraham, production specialist

Photo Credits:
All photos by Capstone Studio/Karon Dubke
Background design elements by Shutterstock
Project production by Marcy Morin, Kayla Rossow,
Mari Bolte, Lori Blackwell, and Sarah Schuette

Printed in Canada.
010395F17

Table of Contents

Best Blocks 6

The Greatest Greeting 8

Bottled Bling 10

Sharp Sketches 12

Creative Clay Club 14

Charmed By Clay 17

A Fine Place for Flowers 18

Warm Fuzzies. 20

Hot Pies 21

Yards of Yarn 22

Mobile Knitting. 23

Toe-tally Custom 24

Sock Safari. 25

An Old Favorite. 26

Melt A Bead 27

A Brush with Creativity 28

Home Sweet Home .30

Read More 32

Internet Sites. 32

Maker Space Tips. 32

The passionate crafter can spend hours exploring and reimagining DIYs and how-tos. But what will you do with everything you make and create? Why not share the love? Make someone's day with a piece of art you made just for them. No two projects will come out exactly the same!

Best Blocks

A simple piece of scrap wood can be turned into something great! From wall hangings to desk decorations, these bits of wood will brighten anyone's day.

Steps:

1. Cut a piece of decorative paper to fit your block. Paint a thin layer of decoupage glue over the block. Gently press the paper onto the block, smoothing out any wrinkles or bubbles.

2. Add more decoupage glue over the top of the paper, and let dry completely. Then add more glue.

Variations:

• Skip the decoupage and just paint the block. Gently rub the edges with sandpaper for a more vintage look.

• Decoupage the blocks with pictures instead of paper.

Steps:

1. Paint your chosen piece of wood. Let a little of the natural wood show.

2. Add a thin paint strip in a contrasting color along the top and the bottom of the wood.

3. Use a pencil to lightly sketch a word. When it's to your liking, fill it in with a dark color.

4. A light color along the edges of the word can really make it pop! Add dots, dashes, or just solid lines when the word is dry.

5. Use the space beneath the word to show off your art skills! Paint something that means something to you. Hearts, feathers, or paw prints are just a few ideas.

Variations:

• If you don't have a steady hand, use stencils to paint on a name or a message.

• Paint several blocks or wood pieces of various sizes. Choose coordinating colors and patterns. Display them by stacking or hanging them together.

• Give your block a more 3D look by gluing on wooden letters or shapes instead of painting on words.

7

The Greatest Greeting

No matter how thrifty you are when it comes to cutting, there always seems to be paper left over. Hang on to favorite designs, prints, and textures and make some custom-made cards. Then use them to drop your besties a line!

How to:

Use pieces of scrap paper to create the ultimate mini scrapbook. Cut pieces into squares and rectangles of various sizes, and arrange them on the front of a greeting card. Play around with patterns and color themes until everything is to your liking. Then glue pieces into place.

Variation:

• Trace or sketch a design from a book cover or illustration onto sheet music or a book page. Then cut your design out. Glue it onto a thin piece of cardstock for the ultimate bookmark.

Tip: Use a thrift store book, or just photocopy a page from one of your favorite stories.

Variations:

- Cut pieces into geometric shapes, such as triangles or hexagons. Fit pieces together like a custom-made puzzle. Scrapbooking scissors that can cut in scallops, zig-zags, and other decorative edges can add some extra fun to paper pieces. Or, use an actual puzzle as a template and cut the paper into puzzle pieces instead!

- Use a small round hole punch and cut out a pile of colorful circles. Arrange the circles on the front of a card. You can overlap the pieces, or you can space them evenly.

- Don't feel like you have to make a card! Decorate a box, a notebook, a canvas, or anything else you can imagine! A layer of decoupage glue over the top of the completed project will keep paper corners flat and add some durability.

- Washi tape is another craft supply that always seems to sit around. Use it like you would regular paper. Try layering the washi with the paper. Why not add a weaved design on bookmarks underneath your paper cutouts? Or mix bold strips of tape with smaller accents of paper.

Tip: Leave a pre-printed message! Type a message in a word processing program. Gently attach washi tape to a piece of printer paper. Try to line the tape up with where the text will print on the page. Place the paper in a laser printer, and print your document. The ink should adhere to the tape, and the tape should easily pull up to be repositioned on your card.

♥ TRY IT!

hello friend

9

Bottled Bling

Find your friends at the gym every time when they're carrying around blinged-out beverages!

How to: Use industrial-strength glue to cover your bottle with flat-backed rhinestones. Let the glue dry completely before using.

Steps:

1. Cut a piece of glittery vinyl long enough to wrap around your bottle. It should be wide enough to cover at least the bottom quarter of the bottle.

2. Place a piece of transfer paper over the top of the vinyl. Rub everywhere the paper touches, especially around the edges.

3. Flip the paper over and peel off the back of the vinyl. Carefully position the vinyl over your bottle, and press into place. Then rub the paper again. This will transfer the vinyl onto the bottle. Gently pull up the transfer paper.

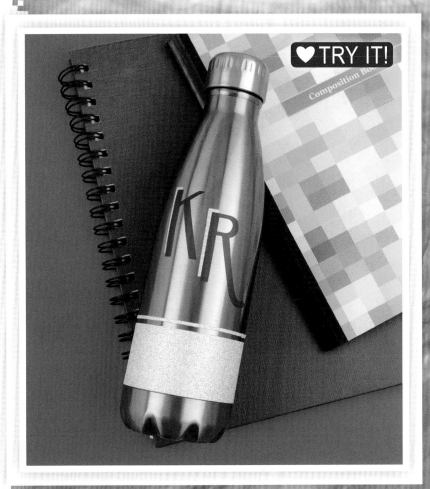

♥ TRY IT!

Tip: To keep your design fresh as long as possible, hand-wash only. A coat or two of brush-on gloss glaze will also help your vinyl last.

Tip: Vinyl placed on rounded surfaces may bubble as it transfers. Use a crochet hook to gently pull up the vinyl to reposition it and get it to lay flat.

Variation:

• Add two or three thin strips of glitter vinyl above the large strip. Leave a small space between each vinyl strip.

11

Sharp Sketches

It's fun to collect permanent markers in every color. Don't let them dry out before you can enjoy them! Find your friends' favorite colors and doodle something that says, "thinking of you."

How to:

Personalize a plain notebook with permanent marker stars, lines, curves, circles, or any other shapes you can imagine. Explore symmetry with mandalas, or try your hand at paisley or floral designs. Make it extra-special by adding a monogram or a favorite quote.

Steps:

1. Use permanent markers to draw in spots of color across a plain white cotton pillowcase. Experiment with a variety of shapes and colors — large, plain spots and simple lines are good starts. Then add small dots, curls, waves, or even simple drawings such as feathers or trees.

2. Once your design is to your liking, pour rubbing alcohol into a spray bottle. Mist the alcohol over the fabric surface. The alcohol will cause the marker ink to run and create a tie-dye effect. Let the alcohol and ink dry completely.

Variations:

• Use black markers (or iron-on vinyl) to write a letter or quote on your pillow. Or use the same technique to create a silhouetted shape, such as an animal or a symbol (like an anchor!)

• Before you start inking, use a hot glue gun to make a design on your fabric. Then follow all the instructions above. Once the alcohol and ink are dry, carefully peel away the hot glue. (If the glue is hard to remove, use a hair dryer on high heat to re-melt the glue a little.)

♥TRY IT!

Tip: If you have just a pillowcase but no pillow, place a piece of cardboard inside to protect your work surface.

13

Creative Clay Club

There's no need to craft alone – why not have a party where everyone can create? Polymer clay is something people of all ages can have fun with. Let guests make their own style of bead or charm. Then let everyone take one of each for a fresh take on friendship bracelets.

Steps:

1. To make basic round beads, pull off a small piece of polymer clay and knead it until it's soft and pliable. Roll it into a ball. Then use a needle to poke a hole through the middle.

2. To add a colorful swirl, roll two pieces of clay into snakes. Twist the snakes together. Then roll the snake into a ball and add your bead hole.

3. With an adult's help, follow baking instructions on your clay package. Keep a close eye on your beads! Once they are baked and cooled, spray them with a polymer clay sealer.

♥ TRY IT!

♥ TRY IT!

Variations:

• Brush on ultrafine glitter before baking. Use a paintbrush to brush off any excess glitter.

• Roll the clay beads in tiny glass beads before baking.

• Gently flatten clay balls into donut shapes or ovals before adding a hole. Use a variety of bead shapes on a single necklace.

• With an adult's help, use a craft knife to make random cross-hatch patterns along the main surface of the beads. Once the beads are baked and cooled, gently sand the outsides, or sponge with a light layer of acrylic paint. Then seal.

♥ TRY IT!

- To make beads for thick metal bracelets, use a knitting needle to poke a large hole in the beads. Press metal eyelets into either side of the hole.

- Roll the outsides of a circle to taper the ends of a round bead.

- For a thick layer of glitter, brush beads with liquid clay and then roll in glitter before baking.

♥ TRY IT!

♥ TRY IT!

Tip: Polymer clay comes in many colors. But you can also color your own clay by using translucent clays. Mix them with crayon bits, mica powder, powdered pastels, or embossing powder.

Charmed By Clay

1. Press a ball of clay into a flat pendant. Use a straw to cut out a round shape near the center of the circle. Use a wire to make a hole that goes from one side of the flat circle through the cutout, and then out the other side.

2. Roll the reserved clay you cut out into a bead. Make a hole in the round bead too. Bake both pieces as directed. When you string your beads, string the round bead so it's centered in the pendant's hole.

Variations:

• Use a regular bead or gem instead of making your own out of reserved clay.

• Make this into an ornament or a keychain instead of a pendant.

• Create a design in the flat clay with stamps and ink.

17

A Fine Place for Flowers

Whether you have a green thumb or just like the idea of plants, flower pots are easy to come by. Fill them with fresh flowers for a May Day or birthday surprise.

Steps:

1. Give your pots a reverse-drip-dried look! Use acrylic paint to color your pot, if you want. If your pot has a hole at the bottom, cover it with a piece of tape. Then turn it upside down over a well-protected work surface. Use a drying rack, pieces of wood (such as chopsticks or wood scraps), or upside-down cups to keep the edges of the pot off the ground.

2. Squeeze out some acrylic paint out over the center of the pot's bottom. Repeat with additional colors of paint. Continue adding paint until it drips over the edges of the pot. You can stop now and let the paint trickle down the pot, or you can keep adding paint to cover the entire pot. Whenever you are satisfied with your paint drips, you can stop and let your pot dry.

3. Flip the pot over and sand off any rough edges near the lip of the pot. Seal the pot with acrylic sealer to protect the paint.

Variations:

• With an adult's help, spray paint your pot any color you like. Use industrial-strength glue to attach flatback gems to the pot. Once the glue is dry, coat the entire pot with spray paint again.

• Use balsa wood, tiles, bits of broken pots, or sticky-back foam instead of gems.

• Skip the paint, and glue the gems straight onto the pot. Use a variety of colors.

Tip: For an extra pop, paint the inside of the pot a bold, solid color.

♥ TRY IT!

Variation:

• Celebrate the Day of the Dead with festive sugar skull pots. Paint your pot white. Then choose where your face will be, and paint two large eyes. Add a nose and mouth. Then create symmetrical designs including loops, swirls, and dots. Add splashes of color, and use fine-tipped brushes for fine details.

Tip: Sugar skulls are decorated to celebrate a person's life. You can find a lot of design inspiration online. Spend time learning about Mexican heritage — you might learn something new!

Warm Fuzzies

Heat up your friends' hands (and hearts!)
by giving them the warm fuzzies.

1. Use a marker to trace or draw a freehand circle onto a piece of brown fleece. Cut it out. Cut out a smaller circle in the center. Repeat with a second piece so you have a front and a back.

2. Cut a smaller circle out of burgundy fabric. Cut a circle out of the center. Use scissors to make the outside edges wavy.

3. Stack the burgundy fabric onto a brown circle. Line the center circles up, and sew them together.

4. Pin the two donut pieces together. The burgundy fleece should face in. Sew all three layers of fleece together along the inside circle.

5. Pull the plain brown circle through the center hole.

6. Sew along the outside edge of the brown circles. Try to stitch as close to the edge as possible.

7. When you have just a small bit of the outside left unsewn, fill with dried corn, flax, or rice — all materials that are safe to warm.

Variations:

• Use embroidery thread for color contrast.

• Upcycle an old flannel shirt, sweater, or leftover fabric instead of using fleece.

• To use your hand warmers, just heat in the microwave for 30 to 60 seconds.

• Add a few drops of your favorite essential oil for a nice scent.

Hot Pies

Make hand pies that are (almost) yummy enough to eat. These cheerful warmers are just one way you can put your own spin on a sweet surprise.

Steps:

1. Use pinking shears to cut circles out of light brown fleece. Cut another round shape with curved edges using white, brown, or pink fleece for frosting. Glue or sew the frosting onto one circle. Add long, thin beads for sprinkles. Use more beads or a permanent marker to make faces.

2. Stack the circles on top of each other with the frosting facing up, and stitch together before filling.

Variation:

• Make a fleece bag to store your hand warmers. Measure and cut two pieces of fleece 9 by 18 inches (22.9 by 45.7 centimeters). Stack them right sides together, and sew down the short edges. Turn the fabric right-side-out, and fold in half with the liner on the outside. Sew up the sides of the bag. Then turn it inside out. Glue or sew hook and loop fasteners inside the bag near the top to keep it closed.

♥ TRY IT!

Yards of Yarn

Did you know color can boost your mood? Logic would say that lots of color pops could turn a bad day completely around! Use up yards of yarn and make someone smile at the same time with these bright pom-poms.

Tip: To make many pom-poms at the same time, wrap yarn around the back of a chair instead of a fork. Tie loops every inch around the wrapped yarn. Then cut between each loop.

Steps:

1. To make a small pom-pom, gently wrap yarn around the tines of a fork between 90 and 100 times. Cut off the end. Loop a piece of yarn between the center tines and tie it tightly around the yarn to make a bow shape. Cut off the excess yarn.

2. Slip the yarn off the fork and cut the looped ends with scissors. Use the scissors to trim the yarn into a round pom-pom shape.

Mobile Knitting

Hang the perfect present for the yarn lover in your life! They'll want to display this mobile masterpiece everywhere.

1. Cross two knitting needles, and use yarn to hold them in place.

2. Make tiny yarn balls by gluing the end of some yarn to a small craft foam ball. Wrap the yarn until the entire ball is covered. Use a small dab of glue to attach the tail end of the yarn. You can make larger balls by using larger foam balls, or adding more yarn.

3. To make mini knitting needles, glue a small, round bead to one end of a toothpick. Repeat to make a second needle. Carefully skewer the toothpicks through the yarn ball. Trim the toothpicks to the appropriate size, if necessary.

4. Tie a 6-inch (15.2-cm)-long piece of fishing line to a yarn ball. Tie the other end of the line to the knitting needles. Continue hanging yarn balls on the needles, varying the length of fishing line.

Variations:

• Use pom-poms instead of yarn balls.

• Make a garland instead! Tie yarn balls or pom-poms together with a single long piece of fishing line. Leave a little space in between each ball, or push them tightly together. You could also make a necklace. Try alternating pom-poms with beads or smaller poms.

23

Toe-tally Custom

Fabric paint is the easiest way to customize clothing. Test out new techniques on socks, and give them away as sleepover, sports, or spa gifts. Then take it to the next level—replicate your designs on shirts, blankets, towels, pillowcases, and anything else that's fit to print.

How to:

Decorate the bottom of your favorite socks with puffy paint. Let the paint dry, and you'll have the grippiest, most slip-proof socks ever.

Variation:

• Use a stencil and regular fabric paint on the bottom of your socks. Try something fun, like hoofprints, rainbow stripes, or pawprints!

• Get more attention with a fully-decorated sock. Draw a V-shape on both the inside and outside of the sock to make a monster mouth. Add teeth, and then add any kind of monster you can think of! Sharks, crocodiles, dinosaurs, piranhas, and dragons are just a few starting ideas.

• Skip the teeth and go with snakes, frogs, fish, or whales instead.

♥ TRY IT!

Sock Safari

How to:

Try out basic tie-dye with fabric spray paint. Protect your work surface with newspaper to prevent the paint from soaking through. Turn an empty soda can upside down on your workspace. Pull a sock over the can. Scrunch the fabric, varying the size of the folds and the space between each. Then spray the sock with paint. Use plenty, for the best color coverage. Let dry completely before wearing.

Tip: Wash and dry socks before painting them. Follow the instructions on the fabric paint's label for directions on drying and aftercare.

An Old Favorite

Friendship bracelets are a classic gift to give. And because pony beads come in such a wide range of colors, you can customize bracelets for each person. But bracelets are just the start of what you can do with pony beads!

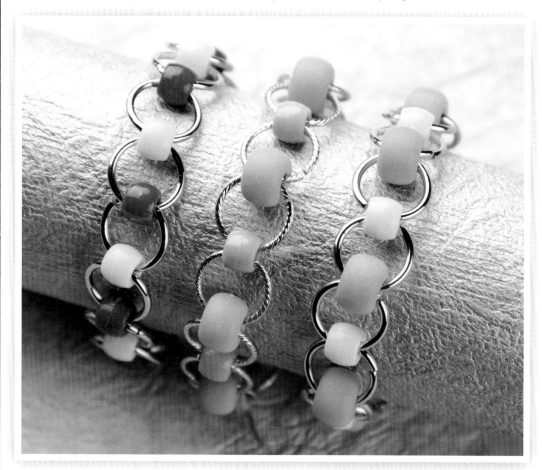

How to:

String two pony beads onto a jump ring. Close the ring. Continue alternating beads and jump rings until the string is as long as necessary. Use a final jump ring to join the pony beads at the ends of the bracelet.

Variation:

• Add small seed beads onto the jump rings for a more feminine look.

Melt A Bead

Steps:

1. You can also melt pony beads! Place a metal cookie cutter on a baking sheet lined with parchment paper. Set a smaller cookie cutter inside the larger cutter. Pour beads to fill the outline of the large cutter.

2. Have an adult preheat a toaster oven to 400 degrees Fahrenheit (205 degrees Celsius), and bake the beads until they melt. Have an adult remove the baking sheet, and let the beads cool.

Tip: Go outdoors! Plug in the toaster oven in an outdoor outlet, or use an outdoor barbecue grill on high heat. The fumes from the beads can be hazardous in an enclosed area.

Variations:

• Place the small cookie cutter near the edge of the large cookie cutter, instead of in the center. When the beads have cooled, wrap bracelet wire along the edge of the ornament. Add beads for some interest.

• Instead of the small cookie cutter, place small metal beads around the outside of the large cookie cutter. The metal beads won't melt, and you can use the beads' holes for hanging your ornament.

• Sprinkle the hot melted pony beads with small seed beads.

• Make a BFF version by making a smaller charm out of the small cookie cutter. Give away the large piece, with the small cookie cutter's shape cut out, and keep the small cookie cutter charm for yourself.

A Brush with Creativity

No art room would be complete without chenille straws. Bend, roll, twist, and wrap projects that you'll actually want to give away as gifts.

Steps:

1. Protect your things by adding some metal armor in disguise. Roll chenille straws into flat circles, and use glue to keep the ends in place.

2. Trace and cut out a felt circle. The felt should be the same size as the chenille circle. Attach the chenille to the felt.

3. Continue rolling, cutting, and gluing until you have enough circles to cover a tote bag.

4. Start at the bottom of the bag, and glue on a row of circles. Overlap the next layer of circles with the first, to create a scale effect. Keep gluing until the whole bag is covered.

Variations:

• Paint chenille straws with sponges. Dab for a subtle effect, or paint the whole chenille straw to broaden your color choices. Add texture and details with permanent markers.

• Twist two chenille straws together before rolling them for a swirled effect.

• Use hot glue to attach one end of the twisted chenille straws to a glass ornament. Continue wrapping and gluing until the entire ornament is covered.

• Thread beads onto the ends of the chenille straw before you start twisting.

♥ TRY IT!

Home Sweet Home

Sometimes you don't need to visit the craft store to find amazing art supplies. Tile spacers, landcaping sand, and glass blocks are cheap and easy to find in any store's home improvement section. Or look around your own house — maybe there's something you can use to make a meaningful gift for a friend who's moving away.

How to: Construct something great with tons of tile spacers. They're sold in large bags and are inexpensive — but ask around first. Maybe someone has extras!

Use tile spacers to make a frame for flat plastic picture holders. Line them up for a picket fence look, or overlap them for something more abstract. Industrial-strength glue will hold everything together.

• Try using spacers everywhere! Use as a backdrop for aquariums, or as a border for a mirror.

♥ TRY IT!

• Sand is often used for landscaping projects. But it can be used in other ways too! See if you can get your hands on some to make a frame that changes with the tides.

• Stir white glue and sand together until the mixture is runny. Use wood craft stick to spread sand along the edges of a frame. Let this layer dry for about an hour. Add another layer, using the stick to create drips and smears. Repeat a third time, if desired. Then let the sand dry completely.

♥ TRY IT!

Steps:

1. Try another fixer-upper from the home improvement store — glass blocks! Clean the glass with rubbing alcohol before starting. Then use permanent markers to create a masterpiece in the style of stained glass.

2. Once your design is just how you want it, brush a layer of decoupage glue over the glass. Let it dry completely. Then re-color your design. Add another layer of decoupage.

3. Continue coloring and decoupaging. The more layers of marker, the deeper the color will be. When you're done layering, outline your edges with black or metallic permanent marker.

Read More

Chenevert, Pam. *Make It Yourself! Paper Pop-Up Art!*.
Minneapolis: ABDO Pub., 2017.

Meinking, Mary. *Start Your Crafting Business*.
North Mankato, Minn.: Capstone Press, 2017.

Suen, Anastasia. *Birthday Gifts*.
Vero Beach, Fla.: Rourke Educational Media, 2017.

Internet Sites

Use FactHound to find Internet sites related to this book.
Visit www.facthound.com

Just type in 9781515773740 and go!

 Check out projects, games and lots more at
www.capstonekids.com

Maker Space Tips

Download tips and tricks for using this book
and others in a library maker space.

Visit www.capstonepub.com/dabblelabresources